# WINNING STRATEGIES

## FOR MICRO, SMALL & MEDIUM ENTERPRISES (M.S.M.Es.)

Written By, Edward Alphonso Harris QBE; Sm; SM, MR&A
Dips, London; Biblicist, Business & PR Consultant,
Real Estate Broker, Networker, Freelance Journalist,
Motivational Speaker, Small Business & CSR Advocate

Even in the best of times 85% of MSMEs fail
This book is your Passport to being in the 15%!

*Dedicated to Students, Employees
& Business Practitioners*

## LIST OF SPONSORS

The publication of this book was made possible with the kind sponsorship of the following companies.

Alpha Innova Group – Hired Caribbean
Anthony's Electro – Mechanical Services Limited
Baron Foods Limited
Construction & Industrial Equipment Limited (CIE)
Essential Hardware Limited
Flavours of the Grill - Forest Spring Limited
Gafsons Group of Companies
-        Gafoor's of Guyana
-        Barbados Steel Works Limited
-        Grenada Steel Works Limited
-        Essential Hardware Limited
-        New Frontier Industries Limited

Icon Security & Investigative Services Limited
Mc Dowall Broadcasting Corporation (MBC)
New Frontier Industries Limited
O. L. Davis & Company
Priscred Limited
Saint Lu Metal & Plastic Manufacturers
S & K Manufacturing Limited
Stone Culture Limited
Theobalds & Associates
U Wash & Dry Cleaning Services
Walker & Company Limited
Forest Spring Limited
Published by Edward A. Harris,
Place of Publication – Castries, Saint Lucia

Published – August, 2016

*DISCLAIMER*
*This book is designed to provide information in regard to the subject matter covered. It is written with the understanding that the author is not engaged in rendering legal, accounting, investment or other professional services. If legal or other expert assistance is required, the services of a competent professional should be sought. The writer is in no way involved in the sale of any product offered in the websites listed in this book and is used only as reference or information relevant to the specific topic. It should be further noted that this book is intended to share the experiences of the author and offers no guarantee for the success of its readers. The Author accepts no responsibility for any website that may no longer exist at the time of purchase of this publication.*

**Designed & Printed by The Office Authority Ltd.**

# ACKNOWLEDGEMENTS

This milestone was made possible because of the encouragement I received from my family, colleagues in the private sector in Saint Lucia and beyond. It would be amiss of me, if I failed to recognize the special relationship I shared with Tedburt Theobalds and Priestley Louison, over the years, as we struggled to establish a voice for the Micro, Small and Medium Enterprises (MSMEs) sector in Saint Lucia, and with Jonathan Adams (deceased) of Trinidad and Tobago as we ventured into CARICOM.

I will never forget those persons/companies that gave me the opportunity over the years to further expand my career here in Saint Lucia. It began with Mr. Stanley Mullings, Managing Director of Stanthur Company Limited (deceased) who invited me to join his company. Later, there were Star Agencies Ltd., Chemical Manufacturing and Investment Company Limited, The Roserie Group of Companies, Baron Foods Limited, Destiny Group of Companies, S & K Manufacturing Limited, Construction & Industrial Equipment Limited (CIE), and Gafsons Group of Companies, including Essential Hardware Limited, Saint Lucia.

My gratitude is also extended to all those whom I have not mentioned specifically, but have contributed in various ways to my achievement in writing and publishing this book.

The Author acknowledges the work of the CARICOM Secretariat and the OECS Secretariat for extracts used in Chapter 4, Pages 22 - 28 and further recommend www.caricom.org and www.oecs.org for further information regarding the work of the Community.

*Edward A. Harris*

# CONTENTS

# PREFACE

This book is dedicated to all those persons who seek to break loose from the pains of poverty and seek their financial independence, through owning their own businesses. Whether you are handicapped by insufficient finance or have adequate start-up capital for your business, the same level of discipline and knowledge will be necessary.

I am very much aware of the volumes of books that have been written on the subject of Small Business Start Up, Development and Management. However, I made the conscious decision to take a different approach and share my personal experiences, highlighting the many obstacles I encountered along the way in my more that 55 years of active involvement in the private sector in Guyana and the Caribbean.

The path to achieving success in business begins with a mindset, which is based upon information and education about the implications of business and a passion to succeed. In this age of information technology, the path to establishing a successful business is well documented. There is no lack of information on how to develop a business and take it through its stages to being successful.

My objective in this book is to present to my readers a holistic approach to developing and maintaining a successful business. The information provided herein is not limited only to my personal experiences and successes but also shares my several failures along the way, especially failing to do the necessary things for achieving success.

I wish to address specifically the operations of the MICRO, SMALL and MEDIUM ENTERPRISES (MSMEs) within the private sector which account for as much as eighty five (85) percent of the workforce in some countries. The private sector is referred to as the engine of growth but MSMEs are the engine of employment. Many governments fail to give the level of support necessary to this vitally important segment of the economy.

I invite you to journey with me as we navigate a path towards understanding the peculiarities, intricacies, technicalities and strategies employed in the operations of MSMEs globally but the Caribbean in particular. Cultures may differ, but business speaks an international language whether you are in an underdeveloped, less developed or developed country.

It is my sincere wish that all persons reading this publication, especially employees who in our modern society seem to be at war with their employers, will get an understanding of the challenges involved in managing a business. I am convinced that a lack of understanding of what it takes to be in business among employees is largely responsible for the state we find ourselves as business leaders and owners. I am fully convinced that every worker has the potential to be a business owner, surely many will. I exhort them to be the best example in their actions as they strive to equip themselves with the discipline and skills that will turn their entrepreneurial dream into reality - when they in turn will expect nothing less than commitment from their employees. Nothing but the best will do!

I am delighted to share my experiences with you. It is my fervent wish that you will take action on whatever business idea that resonates with you. I present to you what I consider to be winning strategies for MSMEs – Enjoy!

You are invited to visit my archive of approximately 400 articles: www.stluciasimplybeautiful.com

# CHAPTER 1
## LAYING THE RIGHT FOUNDATION

The prerequisite for a proper foundation is that it be built on solid ground. It is necessary in every situation where it is important to establish stability, whether it is in a relationship, a physical structure or in business.

It is important to do it right the first time, especially when it relates to business. There should be no room for trial and error, as the result can be disastrous. To ensure the level of excellence that a proper foundation demands, you must have a disciplined approach to life and your business. Discipline is one of the most important ingredients for success.

The need to lay the right foundation in any structure is of paramount importance to achieving success. You must plan to succeed. An important aspect of your journey will be the knowledge you acquire before you begin your journey and a strong commitment to continue to seek knowledge thereafter.

- Don't assume anything – prove all things.
- Take every step, conscious of the implications.

You will be expected not only to gain knowledge about business but also to apply it. Knowledge is power, only when it is applied.

You must be able to answer this very important question – "What is the purpose for your venturing into owning your own business?"
Go to a quiet place in your home or lock your office door and with pen and paper write down what you conceive to be your real PURPOSE for wanting to get into business.

Sometimes, it could mean stepping out of your comfort zone. This exercise is also recommended for persons who have already started their businesses but missed the opportunity due to the challenges and excitement that overtook them as they ventured into being their Own Boss. It is never too late to mend even if it means dismantling the original structure if you have the courage to restart the process, utilizing the fundamentals that have worked for many successful business persons. You can remove the clutter of confusion by rewinding and starting all over again with the approaches suggested in this book in an effort to get it right and increase your chances of sustained success.

You are invited to visit my website where I share some ideas on Affirmation and Goal Setting:
www.brainstorminggroup.webs.com

# CHAPTER 2

## ADOPTING THE RIGHT MENTAL ATTITUDE

Nothing can stop the man with the right mental attitude - Thomas Jefferson

The need for the right mental attitude is indispensible to achieving success in life and in business. This all important fact cannot be over emphasized. There are many BUZZ WORDS that are introduced from time to time. Do you remember "Paradigm Shift" and "Transition"? These steps can only be taken if you accept the fact that you cannot continue to ignore the realities of the current environment in which you operate. You cannot continue to do the same things over and over, expecting different results. It is time you wake up to the fact that the only "Constant" is "Change".

The right mental attitude is a direct result of your thought process where you must deliberately set out to be in tune with the times, be fair in all your dealings and uphold the highest ethical standards in your business. It must be your principal objective to exceed expectations and make a difference.

While for you to be a success in business there must be an element of greed (intense desire), it must be an ethical greed. You must seek to achieve more but not at the expense of others. That is why I embrace the Four Way Test of Rotary International, that is:-
1.    Is it the truth?
2.    Is it fair to all concerned?
3.    Will it build goodwill and better friendships?
4.    Will it be beneficial to all concerned?

The ethical standards I pursued up to the time I was introduced to Rotary were reinforced when I was introduced to the Four Way Test which became my mantra. I sincerely recommend the Four Way Test as the guide in forging your social and business relationships.

You will be greatly assisted when you commit to spiritual values in your business. Don't be caught up with the glamour that comes with being your Own Boss but rather be mindful of the service you render to your customers and the public at large. It must never be all about YOU, Your Wife and Your Children, in isolation to your business associates, your employees and the wider community. You will function best when you are conscious about your environment and recognize your interdependence.

These are the characteristics that define the right mental attitude.

When you establish ethical values in your mind, you will be better able to deal with the issue of MONEY. You will honour your financial obligations fairly and in a timely manner. You must watch your credit rating. It is the one reference you should not treat passively, especially if you want to do business internationally.

With the Right Mental Attitude you will be focused, always seeking to do what is right. Your sub conscious mind will keep you on course.

Be right with your mind and you will be right with the world!

You may ask the question – "What does the right mental attitude have to do with my wanting to be My Own Boss?" Truthfully – EVERYTHING!

Make EMPATHY the watch word that will guide your actions.

# CHAPTER 3

## THE NEED TO ESTABLISH RELATIONS WITH PROFESSIONALS

## *SUCCESSFUL ENTREPRENEUR

Establishing a relationship with a business person who has been there, who has done that with a successful track record and who has survived failures could be one of the most important relationships that someone entering into business can have. Even those persons who have gone ahead and have established businesses and suffer from the fear of seeking advice, due to having to share information about their operations, should in their best interest seek to forge alliances with their successful counterparts.

Business persons need to share experiences and best practices. Joining private sector associations, like the Chamber of Commerce, Manufacturers Association, Small Business Association, and Employers Federation will greatly assist in forging relationships. You may find that established entrepreneurs may even suggest certain types of businesses for your consideration and in some cases propose Joint Venture relationship with budding entrepreneurs who come up with viable propositions.

## *BUSINESS CONSULTANT/MENTOR

This person knows about the importance of the functions being undertaken by the other professionals listed herein. It may be great to start with his/her recommendations as you seek out the services of the others. While you are not supposed to ask the Business Consultant/Mentor about his/her clients' businesses, he/she is very likely to respond to your request to provide you with ideas and recommendations that could be very helpful. You will need his/her assistance in the preparation of your BUSINESS PLAN, one of the most important documents required in starting up a new business. In today's world every lending institution demands a Business Plan.

Do not hesitate to share your vision with your trusted Business Consultant.

## *ATTORNEY AT LAW

You should be guided always by the advice of the Attorney you choose to represent your personal and business interests. You may decide to separate these two interests and deal with different attorneys. The Corporate Attorney will offer you guidance with regards to registering a business name or forming a company, applying for licences, and proper preparation of contracts, forms or other documents that you may require to protect yourself and your business.

## *TECHNICAL/INDUSTRIAL PROFESSIONAL

It will be necessary to establish a relationship with a technical professional, especially if you will be involved in the area of manufacturing where plant and machinery will be employed.

## *ACCOUNTANT

This is a key person in your business. You should develop trust and be mindful of his/her recommendations. You need to develop a close relationship with your Accountant.

- Discuss your plans in detail with him before you commit finances.
- Do not rush to buy that new car or property without discussing with him/her, how you will pay for it. There are many hidden costs in acquiring assets that you will need to take into consideration.
- Planning for taxation, employee benefits, investment of the business surplus income, all need careful planning and administration with the assistance of your Accountant.

## *MARKETING & PUBLIC RELATIONS SPECIALIST

This is the individual who can be very helpful in providing you with the various trends in your market - What's in and what's out. He/she may even be willing to give advice on the types of businesses that are likely to succeed in the existing environment. A Marketing Specialist can also advise you about the best way to inform your market about your business.

Where to advertise, how to get good publicity, how to build an awareness of your business on the internet and how to improve the 'impression' of your business; your logo, stationery, business card, signage all should be well planned to achieve the best results.

## *SOCIAL MEDIA SPECIALIST

If you need results and need it fast, this is the person to engage at the very beginning of your journey. Social Media drives business in today's world. Facebook, Twitter, LinkedIn, You Tube, Instagram, etc. have changed the way business is promoted. Online Marketing in many companies is conducted in a special department, where the Specialist drives massive traffic to the company's website and exposes potential customers to the several irresistible offerings where buying decisions are made.

## *BANKER

The Banker could well be your friend in need. This relationship will need to be nurtured.

Check out your contacts and put them to work for you. They can help you to get an appointment or arrange for an informal meeting with the Business Accounts Manager/Officer of the bank where you propose to establish your business account.

While you might have an established relationship with a bank, where you have developed a track record, that may not be the best bank for your business account. Especially, if you feel that your current bank may not allow you the flexibility necessary to successfully implement your project. But, in business, never assume; put it to the test. Your experience can be different even with the most conservative banker.

There is always someone who knows someone. There is nothing to be scared about.

Bankers are always on the lookout for new clients - get an introduction.

Most importantly, don't just get to know your Banker when you are in need, get your Banker involved with your plans for growth and share your success stories with him/her. This way, he/she knows you, gets to like you and may be more likely to help you, should you ever have a need that requires extending additional facilities.

## *INSURANCE BROKER

An Insurance Broker serves as your one stop shop for all your insurance needs - life, fire, motor vehicle, stock, public liability, employer's liability, etc. The Broker will assist you in getting the best deal (great rates) for your insurance needs and will represent your interest whenever necessary. The Broker will have a direct line to your Insurer.

## *SHIPPING AGENT/CUSTOMS BROKER

Guidance on freight consolidation and shipping can be of great assistance. In recent years many Customs Brokers have expanded their services to include shipping as a one stop shop. Always be on the lookout for excessive Inland Freight cost. Sourcing is important.

Your Broker can help with the costing of your goods. Try to arrive at your final landed cost and the selling price before finalizing the order. A Retail Price Survey can be helpful in assessing the ability of the goods to compete effectively. You don't always have to be the most inexpensive, but you must definitely offer value for money.

## *REAL ESTATE AGENT/BROKER/REALTOR

It is important to develop a relationship with a Realtor. He/she could be very helpful sourcing a great location, and putting some referral fees in your pocket.

## *A SUGGESTED APPROACH TO SELECTING YOUR PROFESSIONAL TEAM

There will be instances where selection of your team might be influenced by your family's association with some of the professionals listed herein. However, you must always have an informed reason for making decisions that set up relationships that should last a lifetime.

You must feel comfortable with such persons. They are your 'business team' and you must feel a sense of confidence and trust in them. But, if you feel the lack of confidence in any of them and/or, that you are no longer getting the professional support that you require then you should not hesitate to discuss this with him/her and if necessary, replace that person/s.

**Networking** is a vital function for achieving success in business. This simple but important aspect of making friends and forming alliances can pay big dividends.

- Do not be afraid to step out of your comfort zone
- Let the world know that you are interested in being an Entrepreneur.
- Genuinely seek the assistance of persons of like minds with whom you come into contact.

You will need to interact with each of the professionals discussed in this chapter in the pursuit of your business. You should try to meet informally first and then make an appointment. That is how great relationships are built. After meeting someone at an informal level, when you meet formally, it is more like meeting a friend - Oh, I remember you!

Each of the professionals mentioned can make a difference in your business. You must create an impression on each of them that you genuinely need his/her assistance in achieving your objective. Most people like to know that they assist others in their climb to success.

You should also seek out opportunities to become involved in service clubs and attend functions where business people are likely to be. For example, if there is a Toast Masters Club in your city or town, you should make it a priority to become an active member for starters.
Visit www.toastmasters.org

Identify a group of persons to be members of your mastermind group. You will be amazed at the level of assistance you can receive from just soliciting advice from professionals and persons in business in general. The greatest asset I feel that is derived from such a group is the reinforcement of your own ideas. Consensus on your proposal will give you greater confidence to go forward.

# CHAPTER 4

## IDENTIFY A BUSINESS IDEA –
## PRODUCT OR SERVICE

## *THE STATE OF THE ECONOMY

The state of the economy is an important consideration in deciding upon establishing certain types of businesses. Timing is everything. There are times when you need to take advantage of the good times, but there are times when a downturn in the economy is also great for investment. So, your timing can be directly related to the type of investment you wish to make.

Remember always that CASH is KING.

Certain businesses do not do well under certain conditions. During 2008 – 2009, the global economic recession impacted negatively on almost every sector. Cash was King. In certain areas of business, for those Entrepreneurs with cash, that was their moment to shine. There is never necessarily a time that is best for entering into business. Opportunities are always beckoning for those who can discern the writing on the wall, so you don't have to sit on the fence and wait for the right time.

In business you must be flexible. Those persons involved in the stock market thrive on declining market prices, as the rule for success is that you buy when prices are low and sell when they are high. However, that doesn't mean investors sit and wait for a crisis.  In the best of times businesses fail. It is for this reason you need to establish relationships with people in business, who walk the walk and talk the talk, who are always looking for new trends as they strive to develop their businesses.

It is very likely that anyone thinking about entering into business will have at least one idea. Here are a few steps to get the ball rolling even when you don't have an idea:

a)  Do a physical check in the streets of the main business centre, look around and see where the business action is, where the customers are spending, and take note.

b)  Do a bit of desk research: use your computer, do a search on your selected business and check out the latest trends and rankings. Suggested question for search - What are the 10 best businesses to invest in today? Find out as much as you can. Use Google, MSN and Yahoo Search Engines.

c)  Check out the import statistics of your country; see where the volume transactions are and just maybe an opportunity will pop out of the numbers.

d)  Check out the Franchise Opportunities on the Internet or get a copy of the Entrepreneur Magazine Top 500 Franchises and see what's hot. Maybe your idea is hot as well.

e)  Talk with owners/managers of successful businesses and ask this question – If you were to invest in a business today, what will it be?

f)  Attend international exhibitions, check out what's new. Be a leader, be first to offer an exciting product or service in your area.

## *WHAT WILL IT BE - A PRODUCT OR A SERVICE?

In the current business environment, all roads lead to the services sector. The warning signals were sent many years ago that the days of the dominance of the agricultural and manufacturing sectors were slowly grinding to a halt. Today, we are witnessing serious decline in the levels of output in these areas, with few exceptions. Many island nations have come to rely almost exclusively on tourism as the major export earner.

The distribution/wholesale sector is moving in a direction of mega warehousing; this is capital intensive which will in time take this activity out of the realm of MSMEs.

The Retail sector will always have space for MSMEs with street vendors, mini mart and small shop operators continuing to hold their own. Already, there are opportunities for small businesses in the retail sector to buy direct, with the importation of 40ft container loads of certain essential commodities such as baby pampers, toilet paper, toiletries, etc. This can be achieved whenever there are truck load specials, close outs, and liquidations from companies, especially in the USA and Canada.

The services sector is where professionals, skilled persons and specialized stores are lining up to take advantage of this emerging sector.

There are many options available to persons seeking to start a business, as well as established Entrepreneurs seeking new areas for investments. Always seek out opportunities to expand within your product category. You will have another product to sell to the customers you are already selling to, thus increasing your sales and ultimately your bottom line.

## *UNDERSTANDING THE ECONOMIC ENVIRONMENT

•        CARICOM Single Market & Economy (CSME) and the OECS Information on CARICOM Single Market & Economy (CSME) and Organisation of Eastern Caribbean States (OECS) Economic Union is very important in setting the foundation for understanding the environment in which MSMEs operate in the OECS and the wider Caribbean region. As Entrepreneurs, you should be aware of the opportunities currently available under the CSME and the OECS Economic Union and use the knowledge to the benefit of your business.

### CARICOM Single Market & Economy (CSME)
### Launched 30th January, 2006

In recent years, the CARICOM Single Market & Economy opened up new possibilities to Entrepreneurs in the region, giving citizens of member States the right of establishment in any State that is a signatory to the Agreement. National treatment is offered and Alien Land Holding Licence which was necessary to acquire real estate by fellow CARICOM citizens is no longer necessary.

While the CSME is not fully operational due to currency implications and other economic matters, the partial implementation of the treaty – CARICOM Single Market (CSM) is slowly advancing.

The total population of the 15 Member States of CARICOM and its Associate Member States is approximately 16,000,000. The Member States are: Antigua and Barbuda, The Bahamas, Barbados, Belize, Dominica, Grenada, Guyana, Haiti, Jamaica, Montserrat, Saint Lucia, St. Christopher (St. Kitts) & Nevis, St. Vincent & the Grenadines, Suriname and Trinidad & Tobago. The Associate Members are: Anguilla, Bermuda, British Virgin Islands, Cayman Islands, and the Turks and Caicos Islands

FACTS ABOUT CSME:

In the Grande Anse Declaration and Work Programme for the Advancement of the Integration Movement, Heads of Government expressed their determination to work toward establishing a single market and economy.

The CARICOM Single Market and Economy is intended to benefit the people of the Region by providing more and better opportunities to produce and sell our goods and services and to attract investment. It will create one large market among the participating member states.

The main objectives of the CSME are: full use of labour (full employment) and full exploitation of the other factors of production (natural resources and capital); competitive production leading to greater variety and quantity of products and services to trade with other countries. It is expected that these objectives will in turn provide improved standards of living and work and sustained economic development.

KEY ELEMENTS OF THE SINGLE MARKET AND ECONOMY INCLUDE:

1. Free movement of goods and services - through measures such as eliminating all barriers to intra-regional movement and harmonising standards to ensure acceptability of goods and services traded;

2. Right of Establishment - to permit the establishment of CARICOM owned businesses in any Member State without restrictions;

3. A Common External Tariff - a rate of duty applied by all Members of the Market to a product imported from a country which is not a member of the market;

4. Free circulation - free movement of goods imported from extra regional sources which would require collection of taxes at first point of entry into the Region and the provision for sharing of collected customs revenue;

5. Free movement of Capital - through measures such as eliminatingforeign exchange controls, convertibility of currencies (or a common currency) and integrated capital market, such as a regional stock exchange;

6. A Common trade policy - agreement among the members on matters related to internal and international trade and a coordinated external trade policy negotiated on a joint basis;

7.      Free movement of labour - through measures such as removing all obstacles to intra-regional movement of skills, labour and travel, harmonising social services (education, health, etc.), providing for the transfer of social security benefits and establishing common standards and measures for accreditation and equivalency.

## OTHER MEASURES:

Harmonisation of Laws: such as the harmonisation of company, intellectual property and other laws.

There are also a number of economic, fiscal and monetary measures and policies which are also important to support the proper functioning of the CSME. These include:

•       Economic Policy measures - coordinating and converging macro-economic policies and performance, harmonising foreign investment policy and adopting measures to acquire, develop and transfer appropriate technology;

•       Monetary Policy measures - coordinating exchange rate and interest rate policies as well as the commercial banking market;

•       Fiscal Policy measures - including coordinating indirect taxes and national budget deficits.

For more information on the CSME, please visit
http://caricom.org/caricom-single-market-and-economy

**OECS Economic Union – An Important Milestone**
The Organisation of Eastern Caribbean States (OECS) comprises of the following States, Anguilla, Antigua & Barbuda, British Virgin Islands, Commonwealth of Dominica, Grenada, Montserrat, Saint Lucia, St. Christopher (St. Kitts) & Nevis, St Vincent & The Grenadines with its Secretariat located in Saint Lucia. It is also worth noting that Martinique is now a full member of the OECS grouping. This relationship came about in April, 2016, opening up opportunities for Entrepreneurs in the tourism and manufacturing sectors.

*Extract from the Feature Address By Dr. The Hon Denzil Douglas, Chairman of the OECS at the Signing Ceremony of the Revised Treaty of Basseterre Establishing the OECS Economic Union Sandals Grande St. Lucian Spa & Beach Resort, Pigeon Island Causeway, Gros Islet, St. Lucia*
*18 June 2010*

### A Proud Record of Success

Since 1981, June 18th has held special significance for us, for it was on that day Twenty-nine years ago, that the Founding Fathers of our Organisation affixed their signatures to the Treaty Establishing the Organization of Caribbean States, commonly referred to as the Treaty of Basseterre after the City in which it was signed. And what a legacy they have left us!

As it marks the beginning of the 30th year of its existence the OECS stands as the leading integration grouping of micro-states in the world. With a total land area of approximately 1000 sq miles and a population of just under 600,000, it boasts a record of success in integration far greater than its physical size and resource capacity would lead one to expect. This success can be measured by the high quality and international reputation of its flagship institutions. For the last forty years, long before the formal establishment of the Organisation, the people of the OECS have benefitted from the operation of a single, fully functional regional judiciary, the OECS Supreme Court. This institution finds no parallel in the world, except perhaps with the European Court of Justice.

Since 1965, long before it was ever contemplated by our friends in Europe, OECS Member States have enjoyed a single currency, the Eastern Caribbean Dollar, which stands today as one of the most stable currencies in the world. It must be noted that our EC Dollar has maintained a fixed rate of exchange to the US Dollar for the past thirty four years! And of course this currency and the entire banking system within the OECS is managed and regulated by a single authority of the highest repute, the Eastern Caribbean Central Bank.

Another institution of long standing is the Eastern Caribbean Civil Aviation Authority, which boasts a successful record in the management and regulation of the airspace and civil aviation within the OECS.

The region's success at integration is also evident in the establishment and successful operation of other institutions of more recent vintage but of equally high international standing, such as Eastern Caribbean Stock Exchange, established upon a platform that is one of the most technologically advanced; or the Eastern Caribbean Telecommunications Authority, the single Authority for oversight of a fully liberalized Telecommunications Sector; or the OECS Pharmaceutical Procurement Service which has realized tremendous benefits for the regional Health Sector through the joint procurement of pharmaceuticals. Indeed, the OECS approach to the procurement of pharmaceuticals has attracted much interest in various parts of the developing world.

And there are yet numerous other successes which the OECS has achieved through pursuits such as joint diplomatic representation in major international capitals and institutions; or policy harmonization and coordination in various spheres of human endeavour including critical areas such as energy, tourism, air transportation, health, education and judicial reform, and foreign policy and trade negotiations.

These successes have resulted in a dramatic increase in the international profile and stature of the OECS, with its development model and success story being promoted internationally to other Small Island Developing States. Additionally, the Organisation's success has attracted the attention of many countries and institutions, with a significant number of them seeking to develop and enter into various forms of closer relationship. Within the last seventeen months alone, six countries (including four from the European Union) have established diplomatic relations with the OECS.

The successes of the OECS are truly amazing when viewed against the backdrop of an international environment that is so hostile to Small Island Developing States. Those of us who are now charged with the responsibility of leadership of this great Organisation owe it to the Founding Fathers and to future generations to guard jealously the legacy which has been bequeathed to us. We have as an imperative, to consolidate the gains that have been made thus far, and undertake the engineering which will place the Organisation on a stronger footing and at a higher institutional level, in order that it could withstand the persistent threats, and the new and emerging challenges that are a hallmark of our time.

## THE MAKING OF HISTORY

Ladies and gentlemen, while we celebrate the past, we have come together in the main, to herald the future - to witness and to engage in, a symbolic reenactment of that afore-mentioned historic event, by affixing our own signatures to the successor Treaty, the Revised Treaty of Basseterre Establishing the Organisation of Eastern Caribbean States Economic Union. This seminal and far reaching document will stand through history as testimony to our maturity as a people, and a testament of our faith in each other and in our collective future. But we are not here engaged in mere symbolism. We are engaged truly in the making of history by meeting frontally, the demands that history has made of us. And even as it makes its demands, history is generous in its offering of lessons and precedent. In 1981 the Founding Fathers of our Organisation were seeking to consolidate the achievements which had been made up to that point through joint action in respect of the governance of the region, and to formalise related institutional arrangements to guide such action into the future.

Please visit **www.oecs.org**

•     European Community Economic Partnership Agreement (EPA) Looking towards the future, Entrepreneurs need to keep in touch with developments taking place with the CARIFORUM-European Community Economic Partnership Agreement (EPA) which was signed on October 16, 2008 but is somewhat lagging behind regarding its implementation. Based on the agreed terms, the private sector stands to benefit from technical assistance and other programmes.

Keep on top of the developments at www.crnm.org

•     **Canada-Caribbean Trade Talks**

Canada-Caribbean Community (CARICOM) Trade Agreement Negotiations was launched – July 1, 2007. Since then seven rounds of negotiations have been held with no end in sight
Keep in touch at www.international.gc.ca

# CHAPTER 5

## YOUR SELECTED TYPE OF BUSINESS - YOUR ROLE?

Manufacturer, Commission Agent, Distributor, Retailer, Service Provider, What?

## *MANUFACTURER

The manufacturing sector with few exceptions is contracting and the future is not encouraging. With the emerging Economic Partnership Agreement (EPA) and America's private sector unrepentant stand on outsourcing to the Asian Block, manufacturers in the CARICOM/ CARIFORUM trading block will be under severe pressure from competitively priced and quality goods from the developed world.

Except for a few areas like condiments, spices, sauces, arts and crafts, manufacturing will continue to be on the decline. Current manufacturers are advised that in cases of their evident demise, to establish relationships with world class manufacturers/distributors to distribute their products in their local markets rather than lose all the time and money that was invested in developing their market share. Private labeling is recommended in cases where the volume of business can justify this approach. It is important to own the BRAND.

The MSMEs sector must also use technical standards in the production of goods and services. These standards are available nationally, regionally and internationally with assistance from internationally assisted agencies such as Caribbean Export. There is also the national Bureau of Standards.

Visit www.carib-export.com

Based on the foregoing, business persons in the MSMEs sector will be left with only one viable alternative, which is, to join their American counterparts and source products from the most competitive sources. This is the reality that business persons in small states will have to face sooner rather than later, except in a few instances where brand loyalty will come to the rescue of some manufacturers. It is advisable that manufacturers do everything to enhance their brand and sustain the interest of their loyal customers in the market place.

Implementation of STANDARDS is the way to go. Do not run from them; embrace them.

## *COMMISSION AGENT

Many fortunes have been made in the past as the persons involved in this form of distribution were characterized as Travelling Salesman, Commercial Traveler, Commission Agent and Manufacturer's Agent/Representative. They were also known as Suitcase Salesmen. Many of these sales professionals travelled extensively within the Caribbean island chain (archipelago). At that time it was a male dominated profession. Today, it is almost the opposite. This method of distribution allowed the Agent/Representative to represent multiple companies which were not necessarily interested in expanding beyond their country or region. In recent times with the introduction of the internet, many companies are using In-house Representatives to sell their products globally. Their efforts are greatly supported by International Trade Fairs/Expos. However, there is always a place for the independent Agent/Representative. A commission of 5 – 10% can be arranged, depending on the product, even higher rates are offered. Business to Business (B2B) has not realized the success envisaged. The Agent/Representative remains a vital part of the process of transferring goods and services from Manufacturer/Supplier to Retailer/Consumer.

## *DISTRIBUTOR

The distribution business has always been an area where opportunities abound. It is simply a matter of finding a product or a range of products that is in demand. Depending on your level of operation and the method of distribution you adopt, it can be manageable with limited capital or become capital intensive.

What will be your channel of distribution? There are several options:
1.  The importer is usually the Distributor who may be appointed an Exclusive or Non Exclusive Distributor. Volume of products to be imported could strengthen the argument for an Exclusive status.

2. Sub Distributors/Wholesalers, who once the product is warehoused will collect from the Distributor and distribute to Retailers. A  Distributor may decide to handle his/her own wholesaling, adopting the Van Sales method while at the same time encouraging Wholesalers to distribute as well. This will depend on the product/s being offered. Find a product that is competitively priced and is in demand and you will be successful. There are certain products that will withstand multiple layers of markups, for example:
a)  Importer/Distributor Suggested Markup on Landed cost 10%
b)  Sub Distributor - Mark up 10%
c)  Wholesaler - Markup 15%
d)  Retailer Minimum Markup – 25%, except on controlled items which can be less and only allow two levels - Wholesale and Retail.
In an open market a Distributor can make three (3) levels (a, b, c) of markups. Wherever there is serious price competition and government controlled prices, distribution markups will be restricted. These are considerations that must be taken on board when selecting product/s to distribute.

There is also the consideration of Price Controlled items, such as cement, where importers/distributors are allowed maximum markups at wholesale and retail levels. This does not mean that the seller cannot sell below the Controlled Price. It was done in the Petroleum Distribution sub sector where a leading Dealer offered prices below the controlled retail price and is also being done by Retailers of cement.

## *RETAILER

This is a relatively simple business but needs a lot of attention. This is the most popular form of business. You will need to employ honest persons to assist you. Small shops are established at almost every corner and are usually passed on from generation to generation. Owners must have a hands on approach.

## *SERVICE PROVIDER

The Services Sector is the fastest growing sector as professionals and skilled persons seize the opportunity to establish their own businesses. Many entrants in business are surprised at how viable their Home Based businesses have turned out. There are numerous niches within the tourism sector which is the lead sector in most Caribbean countries. People with marketable skills are positioning themselves to take advantage of the emerging business opportunities within the services sector.

Take note of the commercial signs that are springing up everywhere. Congratulations to the many young men and women who are now Barbers and Cosmetologists!

With the availability of computers and internet access, the Manufacturers' Representatives and General Commission Agents businesses should be buzzing with activity. Put your computer to use for income generation and seek out opportunities in sourcing products and services. Japanese Used Vehicle business is an interesting area.

On the issue of TERRITORY don't be bashful, request that you or your company be considered for the entire region, not just St. Lucia but all of CARICOM and if you can speak Spanish, you may even include Latin America. In many instances international manufacturers and suppliers don't know and in some cases don't care to know about our geographical location. Go for it!

WHAT WILL BE YOUR SELECTED AREA OF BUSINESS?

You are invited to visit my Facebook Page at:
www.facebook.com/edharrisbiz

# CHAPTER 6

## TYPES OF BUSINESS STRUCTURES

There are five categories of formal business structures that can be considered:-

1.    Sole Proprietorship/Trader
2.    Partnership/Joint Venture
3.    Limited Liability Company - governed by the Companies Act
4.    Co-operative Society - governed by legislation and directly
      supervised by a Department of Government
5.    Public Company – governed by the Companies Act

In the cases of categories 1 & 2, a business name may suffice but it is highly recommended that a Limited Liability Company be established to set up your business as an independent entity separate from yourself. As the name implies, liabilities incurred as a result of the operations of the business will be limited to the assets of the company and not the owner/entrepreneur. Resist at all cost giving unreasonable terms of personal guarantee to your Banker.

There is the suggestion by some professionals that persons should not use their names as part of a business name, i.e.: Edward Harris and Associates, Harris Fashions, etc. The argument advanced is that should the business fail, a stigma is likely to be attached to your name. In my case, my Brand has always been and will continue to be "HARRIS". You decide what's best for you. It is your Name, it is your Brand. It is your reputation. I subscribe to the statement that - Failures are stepping stones to success. The key is that whatever happens – you must always be in business, even it is a passive involvement.

# CHAPTER 7

## NOW THAT YOU HAVE IDENTIFIED THE RIGHT PRODUCT/SERVICE – RECOMMENDED STEPS TO BE TAKEN

It is important that you follow the steps that have been proven to produce results for those persons who have applied the necessary discipline and have become successful.

I can feel the response from some of my readers that many successful business persons have not followed the steps outlined. I beg you to consider how much more successful they could have been by having a well defined approach.  Some people claim that there is method in madness but it is less painful with fewer surprises if you adopt a disciplined approach.

   • Prefeasibility Study will establish if you have identified a business that is viable and whether it should be pursued. You can now test the veracity of your idea by researching it on the Internet.

   • Feasibility Study will test the viability of the project and establish a clearly defined approach for achieving success in your venture.

   • Business Plan will lay everything on the table.  It can be considered the road map to a successful business. All of the component of the business operations will be spelt out in the plan giving justification to your request for financial support. Aspects of the business set out in this document include Preamble/ Background, Experience of the Owner/s, Professional and Technical and other staff, Human Resource Policy, Product/s, Market, Accounting, Cash Flow Projections, etc. In recent times no Financial Institution will talk business with you unless you are fully armed with your Business Plan.

• Marketing and Sales Plan is normally included in the Business Plan but depending on the nature of the company this can be a stand-alone document. I rather like the idea of making stand-alone documents of all the important areas of operation for ease of reference by Directors, Managers and Supervisors of the various departments.

• Budget. The need for budgeting cannot be over emphasised, the Master Budget must be influenced by Departmental Budgets. Even profits are budgeted for as it is the end result of all the operating costs against the projected sales. A budget is a financial document which provides the means through which blood is pumped into the veins of a business. When an Entrepreneur applies the discipline to work within the agreed budget and seek to justify any need for change, he/she is definitely on his/her way to being a successful business person. Monthly review of budget information is of vital importance. Explanations must be provided for Variances whether plus or minus. Month to Date and Year to Date figures with serious comparisons and explanations for the performances under review must be an exercise to keep the train on the track. Always keep your pencil point sharpened.

## STRATEGIC PLAN

Strategic planning can be used to determine mission, vision, values, goals, objectives, roles and responsibilities, timelines, etc. This plan should clearly define the various strategies the business person/company will implement to achieve the several objectives identified. The plan may be for a period of five years but will require constant review which can be scheduled every quarter. It is best done with the Consultant engaging members of the master mind group in the case of a sole proprietor and Directors/Management and selected members of staff in the case of a company with employees.

## A SPECIAL NOTE ON AGREEMENTS:

Make it a point to have a signed agreement in respect of all dealings that are contractual, especially whenever MONEY will not be exchanged until the time of the conclusion of the deal. There has been a serious problem in recent times with getting business persons to honour verbal commitments. When it is time to pay up they always seem to have more commitments than the persons they owe. In the past, it is said that there were instances, where men swallowed IOUs; in today's world, they swallow their verbal commitments, blatantly failing to honour their words. Have you ever heard - my word is my bond? Anyone who makes such a statement should be prepared to respect your wishes and sign an agreement.

I have learnt the hard way and I am at the stage where, if there is no written agreement, I will walk away from the deal. There are many implications such as liability being honoured by the beneficiaries in case of death, and in life if you have no agreement, you have no claim.

Don't rely on witnesses even if other persons were present.
Keep it simple - No agreement, No deal.

It is not easy to get matters tried in the courts these days. Any time you have to resort to the courts, you will be shortening your life due to stress. The emotional stress is not worth it, so stay away from any business that the other party fails to afford you the right to protect your interest.

I am so burdened by this situation that I decided that I must share this plague of dishonesty which is raising its ugly head at a time when everyone needs money. If your customers/clients fail to honour their obligations, how can you honour yours?

## MONEY ALERT!

Cash is King. Without money very little can be achieved. You have to be prudent with money. It is said that MONEY IS THE ROOT OF ALL EVIL but don't be fooled, money is also a source for Happiness and JOY. Give money the respect that is due to it. It is your respect for money that will make you prosperous.

## 1.  BOGUS CHEQUES:

In recent times, there have been a number of scams perpetuated on operators within the private sector. These included fictitious cheques, where persons create cheques with the information belonging to companies and agencies, and forging amounts and signatures on cheques of individuals. In St. Lucia, hundreds of thousands of dollars were lost that way. Be careful in accepting cheques. In accepting cheques from institutions, make sure you get in touch with the Bank on which the cheque is to be drawn. Never be in a hurry to deal with cheque transactions. The Scammers have a unique approach of visiting a sales outlet on a Saturday, when they are fully aware that banks are closed. Be prepared to let the business pass you by. If it was genuine, it will return to you.

## 2.  BOUNCED CHEQUES:

This is a very prevalent activity where persons who are in the possession of a legitimate cheque book go around writing cheques knowing that they do not have the funds to cover the payment. Apply the same precautionary method of checking with the paying institution. This can be very upsetting for a new business with limited cash flow. No business can afford to be a victim of bounced cheques. A person issuing a bounced cheque commits a FRAUD and should be reported to the police immediately. However, in the interest of good relations, try to establish contact with the individual or company first.

## 3.    THE ROLE OF THE BANK:

In recent years opening a bank account is like pulling teeth. It all has to do with our international banking relations and the recently enacted Money Laundering Regulations. While all types of charges were introduced by the Banks in recent times, they have failed to take care of the operators in the MSME sector. In the absence of a National Credit Bureau, something should be worked out to protect the little man, even if it means enacting new legislation. I refer to a small business person receiving a cheque; there should be a clearing house arrangement to protect the Payee. I believe that there should be a method for dealing with the cheque even if it is a paid service, falling under inter-bank transactions.

## 4.    LETTERS OFFERING A SHARE IN A FINANCIAL TRANSACTION:

More than a quarter of a century ago letters inviting persons to participate in moving someone's fortune from a failed state to a safe haven has been in circulation. Although the scam has been well publicized, even in documentaries, people still to this day are lured into this type of scam. Many years ago before the modern day scam of moving loads of cash to a safe destination became popular, there was the chain letter scam and most people got caught in that. First movers always won, they got in on the ground floor. No person in their right mind should fall for such a ploy. Why would someone who does not know you want to share millions of dollars with you? Always remember – if it is too good to be true, then it is.

## 5.    PONZI AND PYRAMID SCHEMES:

Modern day ploy for people from all walks of life. Ponzi is for the movers and shakers and Pyramid is for the little man who gets involved in Multi Level Marketing (MLM) scams. There are good people and bad people in every sphere of life. Business is no exception. I am a firm believer in MLM and am convinced that "MLM is the only hope of the little man" taking a quote from Rod Cook

## 6.    ETHICAL GREED:

Don't get greedy. Don't try to achieve wealth at the expense of others. Be fair in all your dealings. However, this is not to say there should not be an element of greed. I call it Ethical Greed. Wealth is acquired by wanting to achieve more. My grandmother used to say "nothing for nothing, very little for six pence". There is nothing like FREE MONEY. Money is earned in exchange for goods and or services, very seldom it is given away freely without divine intervention and in such situations it is never negotiated. It simply flows from the heart.

## 7.    CREDIT CARD VERSUS DEBIT CARD:

There was a time when Credit Cards were given out without all the demands made upon applicants as exist today. After blatant abuse of the system, Banks are currently demanding Cash Deposit to guarantee Credit Card transactions. The interest rate is very high and every effort should be made to settle transactions promptly to avoid payment of interest.

## 7.   CREDIT CARD VERSUS DEBIT CARD CONT'D:

In the case of Debit Card, you are leveraging your available cash on your savings/checking account with your bank to pay your own bills. Some banks charge a fee for facilitating foreign payments.

In both instances, you must be very careful to keep your Credit/Debit Card safely and effectively supervise its use when being processed by representatives/cashiers of companies you transact business with.

## 8.   WATCH YOUR MONEY:

Never waste, never want. Take care of money and money will take care of you

# CHAPTER 8

STRATEGY FOR FINANCING YOUR BUSINESS

If you plan to establish a business and you have limited resources, you may have to seek external financial assistance. This is the most difficult part if you fail to present proper documented evidence regarding the viability of your business proposition. My advice to persons seeking to establish a business is to approach it as a big business, forget your MSMEs status and do as Entrepreneurs in big businesses do.

Opportunities for sourcing finance:

- Immediate family (on both sides if you are married)
- Friends
- Colleagues at work
- Club Members

Speak with anyone who you think will be disposed to assisting you with raising the needed capital. However, only approach persons identified after careful thought as rejection could be disastrous.

Approach everyone, including family and non family members professionally, and provide documentary evidence

It is your responsibility to be convincing in presenting an honest proposition. My preferred approach is to request a loan instead of shares in the business or entering into partnership.

Offer to pay a premium of between 5 and 10% with flexible terms of repayment becoming due six months to one year after the loan is received.

Make sure you meet your commitments on time.

You may not get all that is needed to give you the opportunity to get ahead with your project without the assistance of a financial institution, but it will definitely assist you to leverage your contribution to get the needed level of capital required to implement your business idea. Depending on the level of financing being sought and your special circumstance, you may wish to consider approaching a Venture Capitalist, Development Bank or ANGEL INVESTOR (a source we hear a lot about in recent times) for assistance.

The issue of companies going public needs some attention. Only established companies can go on the Stock Exchange. Those companies must have successful track records, what about start ups? There is urgent need for a Penny Stock platform where MSME operators can raise capital. We must find creative ways of doing business.

In recent times, we hear about CROWD FUNDING which is promoted on the internet. I know of two companies that have used this form of raising capital. I feel a lot more interest should be developed in this area of raising capital. There are several areas that can be funded through this method, including music. http://www.hongkiat.com/blog/crowdfunding-sites/

Always be certain to make adequate provision for contingencies as many good projects have fallen by the wayside due to lack of adequate startup capital. Bankers do not react well to request for additional funding during implementation stage. Guard against Cost Overruns.

In planning your financial future which should commence on the first day you set out to earn a salary or wage, you should identify at least three financial institutions to do business with, namely, Commercial Bank, Credit Union and Insurance Company. In the event you decide on a business venture, you would have established a track record that could improve the chances of your access to loan funding.

As far as is practicable, never give the Banker more security than is necessary. We live in difficult economic times and through no fault of yours, your business could be ruined. You have seen even banks and solid companies fail in recent times.

Keep close to your Accountant.

# CHAPTER 9

## PRESENT YOURSELF AS AN ENTREPRENEUR

There is a saying "Fake it until you make it". I do not subscribe to such inappropriate statements but I will suggest that "You live your Dream". There are some secrets you need to be aware of as there are sources of influence that you can attract into your life because of the desires you express mentally and spiritually.

- Be informed about the type of business venture that you have selected and be passionate about achieving success in your business.

- Be confident! The easiest approach to succeeding in business or profession is to turn your passion into your business/career.

- You only have one opportunity to make a great impression, do this right and save yourself a lot of frustration trying to regain your standing as the Entrepreneur you strive to be.

- Be well groomed, dress to impress.

The first task upon arriving at your decision to be an Entrepreneur is to get yourself some professionally printed business cards. You must be able to reach for your business card every time you are introduced to someone whom you will like to be in contact with. To be sure that you always have a supply of business cards on hand, place a few in your purse or wallet. Make sure that you select an email address that presents you as a serious business person. Sexygal@hotmail.com or rudeboy@gmail.com is simply unacceptable.

- Be able to speak convincingly about trends and peculiarities in your proposed business, establish your dominance in word and deed.

- Be an avid reader about developments in the area of business you selected.

- Subscribe to magazines such as the Bloomberg Business Week, Time, Entrepreneur, etc.

Attend trade fairs related to your business and subscribe to professional groups on the internet such as LinkedIn (www.linkedin.com), newsletters, forums, etc.

www.linkedin.com

# CHAPTER 10

## IMPLEMENTING YOUR BUSINESS

## *BUSINESS LOCATION

Most persons who have attended business courses would have heard the words – Location! Location! Location! You need to position yourself to be accessible to your customers. This is especially true for the Retail Business. In certain businesses, the actual location may not matter much, but it is always an advantage to have visibility and accessibility when it comes to locating your business. Significant benefits can even be derived by placing your business sign at a great location.

It is important to note that high visibility locations are very expensive and it may be necessary to start where your budget will permit but certainly you will expect to grow. This knowledge could serve you well in the future.

Many businesses in the services sector can easily be established in your home. Home based businesses are greatly preferred wherever practicable as there are many social benefits apart from being cost effective. In some instances discipline will be necessary.

*Infrastructural Works & Equipping the Operations
You can spend a lot of money on this aspect of your business and need to aim as much as possible to keep costs down.
- Stay close to your budget,
- Negotiate everything,
- Ask for discounts,
- Seek out opportunities to buy surplus and used goods, including equipment,
- Most of all - be creative.

## *SOURCING OF PLANT, EQUIPMENT, RAW & PACKAGING MATERIALS & PRODUCTS

This is mostly needed in a manufacturing operation. The Manufacturer, from the time the project is conceptualized, should as an ongoing exercise, seek out the most competitive sources of supplies in keeping with the overall policy of the firm. The Internet has made life very easy as almost any product or service could be sourced online. However, there are imminent risks in dealing on the internet. Never be in a hurry when transacting business online; do your due diligence and even after arriving at a conclusion to do business with a source, finalise the decision after a twenty four hour cooling off period.

I worked for a gentleman who insisted that I should never go to his office for his immediate response to any business proposition no matter how great it might be. While I don't totally agree with such a position, there is some merit in the position which he took. Many of us have established some guidelines for our behavior over the years.

I discovered a long time ago, never to get excited about prices until you sit down with pen and paper and add up all the various contributors to the landed cost. Inland freight and ocean freight can spring major surprises. A very good ex-factory price could be unattractive when the CIF is calculated. There is also the issue of customs levies when importing from a member State of a regional trade grouping as opposed to an extra regional source.

Secure the services of an efficient Customs Broker to handle your shipments once you plan to import, and discuss with him/her the various implications related to the importation of the types of goods you plan to import.

In sourcing machinery and equipment, it is important to decide very early if it will be new or used? There are bargains around the world on used and out of production machinery and equipment due to upgrades and liquidations. Some companies make a business out of refurbishing used machinery and equipment.

It is also important to note that in some cases you can hire a technical service person to evaluate the machinery/equipment that you have identified for possible purchase before finalizing the deal.

## *RECRUITMENT OF STAFF

This is a very important aspect in establishing a business. Employees are your greatest internal asset.
The best recruiter is the person who can put a team together that will be united in their purpose to achieve the best results for the company. No company will achieve its real potential if workers are divided and management has to spend the greater portion of the working hours refereeing battles among staff members. Achieving unity of purpose among employees is the best result any employer could realize. The best approach is for the expectations on both sides to be clearly defined and accepted. This is achieved by an interview where the applicant is allowed to express his/her views freely.

- Take your time to fill the positions,
- Interview as many qualified applicants as possible, and,
- Follow up with an offer of employment letter and include a copy of Job Description and Task Analysis (in duplicate) to successful applicants.

Persons selected will be expected to sign each copy included in the Offer Package and return prior to or on the day of assuming duties.

The time spent in the interviewing process is never wasted and can make a substantial difference in the operations of your company. Do not forget that the induction of an employee is very important so that there can be no misunderstanding regarding the new employee's role.

You will be on your way to being a great business person if you will be guided by the definition given by Peter Drucker – "Management is a social process which entails the mobilisation of human resources for a common objective".

## *EFFECTIVE RECORD KEEPING

Failure to maintain proper records is not in keeping with the behavior of someone seeking to be successful in business. Try to resist the temptation of getting into business with anyone who is indifferent to the idea of keeping records.

As a teenager, I studied Book Keeping at evening classes and the definition of Book Keeping was engrained in my mind, and I quote, – "Book Keeping is the art of recording transactions in such a manner that the financial position of a company can be ascertained at any given point in time" (Routley).
There are several accounting software packages that will keep an up to the minute and accurate record of your business activities. Point of Sale software now used extensively in retail is extremely vital to keeping on top of your business.

Keep it simple, don't be overwhelmed with details.

# *CONFORMING TO GOVERNMENT REGULATIONS

There are numerous regulations such as Environmental, Occupational, Health and Safety, etc. Business persons should seek out the information from the several ministries and agencies that monitor the implementation and adherence to the various regulations. The Employers' Federation in your country should be very helpful with respect to labour matters. In most countries, there is a Labour Code which sets out the terms and conditions of employer/employee relations.

A Government can only provide essential services to its citizens if it collects revenue in the form of taxes. It is the responsibility of every citizen to ensure that he/she pays their fair share; however, business persons should ensure that they work closely with their Accountants to reduce the impact of taxes on their bottom line. There are many fiscal incentives and allowances that can greatly reduce the impact of Corporation Tax on your pre-tax profit, affording you a better net profit position.

It is important to keep in mind that proper record keeping gives you a handle on your business and will definitely enhance the possibility of your success. Every aspect of your business should be able to stand up to verification. Computer Software has made life easy for today's Entrepreneur. In the retail business as the Barcode is scanned and the price is entered unto the cash register, the quantity sold is being taken off the stock record. Maybe, pilfering has become less prevalent. VAT is calculated on all transactions and stored in the POS. However, you can have the best system in the world and you fail to inform and educate your staff, the system will not work in your best interest.

## *INCOME TAX AND OTHER GOVERNMENT REVENUE OBLIGATIONS

Income Tax, National Insurance/Social Security, VAT, Property Tax and Corporation Tax, these taxes are mandatory. They should be paid on the stipulated date as failing to do so will incur fines and possible confinement. Never allow the payment of these obligations to fall into arrears.

## *QUALITY STANDARDS, TRAINING, IMPLEMENTATION AND MONITORING

Standards must not be taken lightly in today's world as there are Standards for everything. The popularity of the ISO 9000 series of Standards began with Companies seeking to streamline their operations by putting into place recording and reporting systems that guarantee consistency. Over time, companies subscribing to the standards culture have secured increased performances both in efficiency and proficiency. There are also national and regional quality and product standards which may be readily adopted by MSMEs.

The buzz continues about the Hazard Analysis Critical Control Point (HACCP) Certification for the food and beverage industries. This certification prepares the participating companies to access export markets and also paves the way for some companies to gain World Class Manufacturing status.

Many Caribbean States, today, boast of their own Bureau of Standards, and there is a regional body to support their efforts. What is very clear is that all the companies that have invested in achieving Standards Certifications are lead industries in their categories. They have also gained recognition at the national, regional and international levels - thus achieving excellence on a global scale. They continue to prosper in spite of difficult economic times.

Visit CARICOM Regional Organisation for Standards and Quality (CROSQ) at

www.crosq.org

# CHAPTER 11

## PROMOTING YOUR BUSINESS

## *PUBLIC RELATIONS

This area of activity could be greatly enhanced by the involvement of management and staff in community related activities. Everyone in the Company should make it their business to seek out opportunities for the company's participation in programmes which will assist in establishing the company as a good Corporate Citizen, cognizant of its social responsibilities.

Good PR creates Brand recognition and ultimately customer loyalty which is very important for a company's survival in today's competitive environment.

PR when effectively executed with regular Press Releases could get the company substantial media exposure for free.

## *ADVERTISING – MEDIA, SOCIAL MEDIA, WEBSITE, BUSINESS CARDS

Electronic and media advertising though expensive could be very instrumental in establishing, expanding and sustaining the leadership position of a company in the market place. MSMEs can see their product/s achieve dominance by applying the right media mix to maintain existing customers and capture new ones.

Electronic media is moving ahead of print media. In recent times digital magazines, newspapers and newsletters have been establishing a presence with a noticeable market share.

Websites are very effective means of promoting all aspects of your business. However, updating of your website is vital in ensuring that the benefits intended are received. Ensure that your website is professionally designed and domain name and webhosting are paid promptly when they become due. Business Cards will assist potential customers to maintain contact with you. Make them attractive and ensure that you include information about your business; sometimes it may be necessary to utilize both sides of the card. A photograph can also be helpful in promoting your business.

## *SOCIAL NETWORKING:

It is now a proven fact that www.facebook.com, www.twitter.com, www.myspace.com, and www.youtube.com, have opened up new avenues for marketers in all industries and home based business persons in particular. I like www.linkedin.com where you can network with professionals in most industries and share industry information including sourcing of products and services.

## *GROUP: INTERNATIONAL EXPORT/IMPORT ON LINKEDIN

This discussion group proves the point that you need to be selective as a business person to ensure that you participate in productive groups: "Mosquitoes kill over 1 million people a year. Would you like to be paid a lot of money to kill them? Extremely profitable business opportunity for people in all countries afflicted with mosquitoes". This was a sensational post on LinkedIn.

I was the second person to respond to the post and later the same day, I followed up with my own post in the same thread –"Are you interested in expanding your market to include the English Speaking Caribbean? Find me a product/s as new and exciting as MosquitoFree and I am ready to do business immediately". I got the most responses from this post since being a member of the group.

## *NETWORK YOUR WAY TO SUCCESS

I have been networking for as long as I can remember. I have benefitted tremendously from meeting people, exchanging ideas, keeping in touch, forming alliances and establishing lifelong friendships.

Never fail to seize an opportunity to meet and greet new people, and open doors to mutually beneficial relationships.

I am so proud to be a Networker that "The Networker" was on the back number plate of my car for many years.
St. Lucia is a small island State that is well serviced by Associations representing the various interests of the Private Sector. Associations include:
St. Lucia Chamber of Commerce, Industry & Agriculture, St. Lucia Chamber of Agriculture, St. Lucia Industrial and Small Business Association, St. Lucia Manufacturers Association, St. Lucia Employers Federation, Realtors Association (Saint Lucia) Inc., Saint Lucia Coalition of Services Industries Inc., etc.

Membership in your sector association presents you with opportunities to meet and network with people of similar interests. If there was ever a time that business persons need to come together and share ideas, it is now. Network your way to relationships and prosperity.

## *EXCEED CUSTOMERS EXPECTATIONS

Everyone is talking about customer service but very little is being demonstrated in the relationship between staff and customers. It is this area that MSMEs could make inroads into larger companies' market share. As an Entrepreneur in the MSMEs sector you can challenge the big companies by doing things differently. Give personalized service. Think creatively.

I have been engaged with small companies that reversed trends where large companies held dominant positions for years in the market place, as in the case of Clorox versus Chemico Bleach in Saint Lucia. Don't be intimidated. Offer Quality and Service of exceptionally high standard in a manner that will exceed customers' expectations. The personal touch is a special weapon for Small business operators – use it.

## *PRICING STRATEGY

In today's market place, as consumers grapple with the high cost of living - Price is a key ingredient. Many companies have encouraged competition by demanding exorbitant prices.

I saw a small businessman in Guyana when I worked with the leading paint manufacturing company take a decision to outperform every dealer in the country by taking a profit of G$2.00 on every gallon of paint he sold, while the other dealers priced their product at 33% mark up. The manufacturer offered a monthly performance rebate on sales volume of $1.00 per gallon. This dealer was turning over thousands of gallons of paint per month and receiving thousands of dollars in incentive performance rebate, plus his $2.00 mark up per gallon.

In the early 90s while working in Jamaica, I was associated with a businessman who established a 10% mark up price structure across the board in his supermarket. The lines were long in front of his building in down town Kingston with customers waiting their turn to shop where the price was right.

There is a disturbing trend in recent times where retailers are taking extraordinary mark up and offering discounts only to those customers who have the ability to negotiate. In some cases SALES have become the norm, with companies offering between 30 and 80% Discount. This is not fair to consumers. How will you feel if you bought an item one day for one dollar ($1.00) and the following day that same item was being sold for fifty cents ($0.50)? Some persons have caught on to the SALE trend and only purchase certain items when there is a sale.

In spite of the current state of affairs as it relates to prices, my prediction is that genuine ethical MSMEs will lead the assault to bring about real competition in the market and cause prices to adjust to realistic levels.

CARICOM now has a Consumer Protection Act which was recently enacted in St. Lucia. Let us see how far it will go to alleviate the pain inflicted upon consumers by unscrupulous retailers.

# CHAPTER 12

## THE GOODWILL FACTOR

## *BE SOCIALLY RESPONSIBLE – BE A GOOD CORPORATE CITIZEN

The Organization of American States (OAS) spent a substantial amount of money in promoting Corporate Social Responsibility (CSR) in the Small & Medium Enterprise (SME) Sector in the Caribbean. Simply put, CSR is about

- Engaging the best management principles with full employees participation,
- Being environmentally conscious,
- Taking care of the environment in which you operate your business, and,
- Seeking out opportunities to improve the standard of living, beginning with the community in which your business is located.

MSMEs should lead the way in being Socially Responsible and help to give hope to people of the various communities in which they operate. However, it simply has to do with the mental attitude of business leaders, regardless of the size of the company.

In recent times, due to limited resources of Governments, request for sponsorships and donations have increased substantially, adding further pressure on businesses. This development demands a more thoughtful approach in selecting which organizations to support. I am a strong supporter of schools. It is my feeling that business persons should seek out opportunities in their communities and get together to make a difference in the quality of life for the less fortunate.

# CHAPTER 13

## BEING YOUR OWN BOSS

Being your own boss is a special privilege which carries certain responsibilities enshrined in all religions. It should be your responsibility to take care of the less fortunate, especially those in your employment. Your social responsibility conscience should not allow you to knowingly and deliberately exploit others.

I firmly believe that it is in giving that you receive, yet another religious principle. I remember very vividly a conversation I had with my then partner when we established a company in the Industrial Estate in Vieux Fort, St. Lucia. It went like this:

"We know what poverty is like, we personally lived through it and I am suggesting that we pay proper wages to our employees, not what is being paid by other small companies and even some larger ones but we should pay wages whereby it will be worth our employees while to come to work"

While I am no longer associated with the company; I am very pleased with the results of that decision which afforded me a special privilege to note the advancement that many of the employees have made over the years. After 30 years the company is still standing.

## *FUTURE INVESTMENTS

Do not try to live up to the expectations of others, except for your customers who expect a certain level of service from you. Do not try to do what is popular. Investing in Bonds, Stocks, etc. promoted by glossy brochures because it is popular, has left many of our Entrepreneurs poorer for their exploits on Wall Street and in some of the capitals of the Caribbean.

I never paid much interest in investing for dividends through the exploits of some other individual or company. Six (6) percent should not be attractive to any business person. I would be better off putting my company's money to work in my business rather than under someone else's control to return a dividend on my investment. As a business person no one should be able to get you a better yield on your money than yourself, except when offerings like Facebook comes along. Any time that it becomes necessary for you to part with your limited cash to give to someone else to invest; you should close shop or find another business or full employment, working for someone else.

- Try to invest in income generating projects,
- Expand within your product/business category as far as possible,
- Try to buy cash, demanding a discount, even when credit is available,
- Negotiate every deal.

## REMEMBER CASH IS KING.

Credit costs more in most cases. Some companies charge for late settlement of invoices. Never take money that is needed in the business to invest in other areas. Too often the business that is the main contributor is neglected with the owner, failing to look inside, instead of looking at unchartered options. Stay focused. Stay away from capital intensive projects in the early stages of your business.

You may consider investing some of your extra cash on property whenever you arrive at such a position in your business. Check with your Accountant.

There is an exception. Bearing in mind that we live in an age where the only constant is change, new thinking emerges all the time. You may get involved in Multiple Streams of Income but those must be low investment businesses. Depending on the nature of your core business, you may have a lot of free time on your hands while awaiting a request from a client. The real estate business is one such business especially in the case of new entrants. My present portfolio of businesses includes Business & PR Consulting, Real Estate, Networking, Freelance Journalism, Business & Motivational Lectures, and Private Sector & CSR Advocacy.

You should only consider diversifying your business portfolio when you have available free time to take on the next business.

## *TIPS FOR SUCCESS IN BUSINESS

### TIP #1

Do not be in business for the sake of being in business. If your business is not giving you the excitement that you expected, it is time to take stock and make a decision to do what is necessary to rekindle your interest or move on. Never be afraid to move on. Failures are lessons to learn from. The more you fail, the more likely you are to succeed, and in no small measure. I am at that stage in my life.

### TIP #2

Business is like a love affair. You must be passionate about your involvement in your business. It is all about adding value. Napoleon Hill speaks about Sex Transmutation. You must demonstrate pride and energy in your business. I would like to suggest that you get a copy of his book – "Think and Grow Rich", which is now available on the Internet for free. You have absolutely no excuse to get your free copy.
**www.eventualmillionaire.com/Resources/ThinkandGrowRich.pdf**

## TIP #3

You will only succeed when you help others to succeed. Selfish success will be short lived and miserable. Sharing and Caring are two important words. Make a difference by sharing your ideas with others in business and social interest groups. Lots of heartaches could be saved by sharing timely information. I am amazed at the amount of valuable information I receive on a daily basis by networking and sharing the ideas and opportunities I have been blessed to receive. You are invited to join my FB Page www.facebook.com/edharrisbiz

## TIP #4

Accept your social responsibility and deliver beyond expectation. You will be a better person and your community will be a better place for everyone. Born Again Christians sow seeds by giving to their brothers and sisters in need. It is normal for Christians who have experienced the amazing results of sowing seeds to give substantial amounts of money to others in need. Start today in some small way, and begin to take note as to how you can help others. Try your best to be a BLESSING!

Be mindful about creating debt. Only borrow for productive purposes, all other transactions should be in cash. Credit costs money. If you build a property for cash you will keep all the interest on the mortgage and have twice as much money in twenty or thirty years.

## TIP #6

Only buy when renting is not a feasible option. It is quite a while since Bridegrooms and their groomsmen are renting their entire outfit. If a man could marry in a rented suit, what else that is available for legitimate rental that he should not rent? The ladies rent too; only they are more reluctant to do so when it comes to their wedding gown as they feel a sense of pride to keep their gown in the wardrobe until death do they part. So they can reminisce. Leasing is a very attractive alternative in many instances. Developed countries have leasing companies for almost anything.  If you like the flexibility of living in various communities, leasing is an option to consider. Get friendly with a Real Estate Agent and get in on the rental deals. There is also the possibility to lease with the option to buy.

## TIP #7

Negotiate everything. If you think that you should negotiate and the seller refuses a discount, don't buy. Due diligence is important. Price surveys are necessary in today's world. The Internet affords you the option of comparing almost anything. Don't be lazy.

## TIP #8

Seek out every opportunity to save, not spend. Reduce costs in your business and in your personal life. Try to achieve more with less.

## TIP #9

Dress to impress. Stand out in the crowd, don't be another person in the crowd. Learn to admire yourself to the point that you can smile with yourself.

## TIP #10

Expand your range of products /services within its category wherever possible. Resist spreading yourself too thin, try to be focused. Take a good look at www.amazon.com  and note how they have expanded their services.

## TIP #11

 Keep up to date with industry developments. Read all you can about your industry, visit trade fairs, etc. Remember - readers are leaders.

## TIP # 12

Set up a belief system and a Master Mind Group. Practice your Faith and develop a group of persons around you who share your vision. Do not be a time waster; put your energies to work and network your way to success.

# CHAPTER 14

## THE IMPORTANCE OF MARKETING - THE 4PS:

Marketing is simply a matter of positioning. It is about having the right Product, in the right Place, at the right Price, with the right Promotion. That's the 4Ps. A winning combination when applied at the right time.

**The Product** must be a product/service for which a demand exists. Don't decide upon a product/service that you feel the consumer needs. It is not about you, it is about the consumer. It must be your desire to fulfill a need. Test the demand for your product. Undertake surveys. Let the consumer tell you what is needed. Never assume.

**The Place** - this does not only to a physical place of business where Location, Location, Location should be your mantra but it also has to do with the method of distribution you implement. Your main task after deciding upon the product is to get it in front of the consumer. If you are distributing sweets, get as many confectionery stores as possible to carry your sweets. Go for saturation in your distribution. If you are selling from a tray, secure a high traffic area to position your tray.

**The Price** – In today's world price is key! Acceptable quality with outstanding service is another winning combination. You must know what is a fair price? If your price comes up more expensive – how can you justify asking the consumer to pay more for your product? In some cases you can only penetrate the market with a better price? When a standard is set for a specific product, it is definitely a price game. Bleach is product where the standard is set.

**The Promotion** – go after your target market. Who are your consumers? What is the best medium to reach these consumers? In some cases it will take a combination of media to reach the targeted consumers. While advertising can be expensive, micro businesses have some special advantages. There are several options for attracting consumers to your product/service – press release, public relations, radio, tv, print, social media, banners, word of mouth, etc.

**A special word on Discounts:**

There is a difference between gross margin and markup. It is especially worthy of note when applying discounts.

Gross Margin or Gross Profit is defined as sales minus cost of goods sold. If a product sells for $100.00 which had a cost of $80.00, the gross profit or gross margin is $20.00. The gross profit ratio or the gross margin expresses the gross profit or gross margin amount as a percentage of sales. Example $20.00 divided by $100.00, the gross margin ratio is 20%.

Markup is used several ways. Some retailers use markup to mean the difference between a product's cost and its selling price. Example, the product had a cost of $80.00 and it had a markup $20.00 resulting in a selling price of $100.00. The $20.00 markup is the same as the $20.00 gross profit. However, the markup percentage is often expressed as a percentage of cost. In our example the $20.00 markup is divided by the cost of $80.00 resulting in a markup of 25%.

Keep an eye on the competition; be aware of what they are doing. Do not follow discounted prices blindly. Do not give discounts because your competitors are doing so, find out what is the supply level in the market place and arrive at a possible reasons for your competitors' action. Maybe, it is cash flow or deterioration of product in storage. Sometimes it is better to sit out the competition and make your right level of profit. It is important to pay attention to discounts. In recent times discounts are at their highest - as much as 80 percent with Store Sale running for months. I am ready to predict that very soon some Retailers will only be selling when there is a sale.

This is an opening for DISCOUNT STORES. Watch your mark up strategy. Keep markups realistic and shock the promoters of discounts with continuous sales every day, not only on Sale days.

There is a mega store in St. Lucia which gives zero discount no matter what quantity of the product is purchased. While there may be specials, there is never a store wide sale.

www.mindtools.com

# CHAPTER 15

## THE NEXT BIG WAVE FOR THE CARIBBEAN - MULTI-LEVEL MARKETING - "MLM"

Since 2008, I have written seven articles in my column "Harris at Large" (www.stluciasimplybeautiful.com) highlighting the virtues of Multi Level Marketing (MLM). This is popularly known as Network Marketing and sometimes referred to as Relationship Marketing. I am fully convinced that this business model will be the answer to the unemployment and under employment issues plaguing nationals of the English Speaking Caribbean. To date, no Caribbean Entrepreneur has seen the business opportunity in the Network Marketing Industry. Timing is everything and it is my humble opinion that there can never be a better time to introduce a MLM company with an electronic product offering, fuelled by technology, especially smart phones. We have all witnessed in recent years the introduction of cell phones and now smart phones which many business persons use as a preferred platform for doing business.

The Entrepreneurs of our region will be wise to follow the advice below:

**ALWAYS TRY TO THINK AHEAD**
When you think ahead of any approaching action you'll always have the advantage. You'll be the winner. Keeping a little ahead of conditions is one of the secrets of business. The time to repair your roof is when the sun is shining. Try to do things before they need to be done. Let your advance worrying become advance thinking and planning. Position yourself ahead of time in the best place for you. When you do what is necessary, all the odds are in your favor. Do the next thing.
Copyright 2008 www.yourdailymotivation.com

We live in an age where information is at our fingertips. There is no subject that has been publicly ventilated that the information is not found on the Internet. Thanks to the team at GOOGLE!
I may be Multi Level Marketing (MLM) fatigued but I keep true to the principles of the industry. Rod Cook said it best "MLM is good – the last hope for the little guy". However, the big guys are jumping in. Warren Buffet and Donald Trump own MLM companies. President Clinton applauds the industry. There is money to be made in the business, and we in the Caribbean need to be a part of it.

---

**IT IS TIME TO REVISIT THE MLM BUSINESS MODEL!**
Published June 10, 2011, Updated 17/01/16
Harris At Large!

**IT IS TIME TO REVISIT THE MLM BUSINESS MODEL!**
Affiliate Marketing, Network Marketing, Relationship Marketing, Multi Level Marketing (MLM), etc., all these methods of marketing have one objective in common and that is to generate sales and provide income that will transform lives, affording participants in the industry FINANCIAL AND TIME FREEDOM. The principal function is selling. So as to avoid any misunderstanding, this article is dedicated to the system of Multi Level Marketing (MLM). It is important to note that MLM removes the need for advertising and puts the promotion of the product or service squarely on the shoulders of the Marketer/Independent Distributor. Wherever possible, a combination of internet and direct word of mouth work best, with the latter being most effective in many instances.

It cannot be over emphasized that Multi Level Marketing is a Home Based Business. It pays at several levels and allows for productive business owners to receive super financial and social rewards which allow them to enjoy the good life. It affords those who get involve and are successful – Financial and Time Freedom.

There is no other industry that has leveled the playing field as the MLM Industry. I know of no other industry that an individual can enter without the usual requirements of a business except with for two qualifications that he or she is prepared to apply the system and do whatever ethical action it takes to achieve the goals set out by the company. All that is necessary is that you find a company that you can trust and offers products/services that you can be proud of and get passionate about sharing the experience with others.

In every industry there are bad apples and it is necessary to apply due diligence to ascertain whether the company and its promoters are reputable. It is very important that you make the right decision about the company that you will be associated with. In the MLM business you do the job once and get paid for a lifetime so it is very important that you step cautiously in aligning yourself with any company. There are companies that have been around for over six decades.

I was able to view at first hand the life style of Networkers when I participated in two annual cruises with Multi Level Marketing high rollers (MLM Millionaires and Experts) on their annual MLM cruise www.mlmcruise.com This year they will be cruising for the 27th time and the Caribbean cruise is scheduled for November 25-December 3, 2016. A few years ago the group passed through St. Lucia. It was on my first cruise that I met Rod and Marcie Cook and I have been in contact with them ever since. Visit **http://www.mlmwatchdog.com** I will never forget a quotation from him and I share it here with you, "Network Marketing is the only hope for the little guy". This quote is much more than words; it is reality to millions of little guys, who in the past and up to today have lived their dreams only because of MLM. MLM will continue to be the only real escape route for the little guy.

The dominance of the MLM industry is not about to be lessened as the big guys are now actively participating in several business opportunities. In recent years, Warren Buffet and Donald Trump have entered the business. President Clinton and other influential persons have applauded the industry. Warren Buffet appears to be on a mission buying up MLM companies. He said "Best money I ever spent".

Now that you have been provided with some information about deciding on the right company and product/service, it is now time to look at a generous compensation plan. There is a lot to know about compensation plans and they can be very complicated but you will understand very quickly as you begin to earn and climb the success ladder. It is important to select a company that its owners have a track record in the industry. Here is an example of dealing with one such company. Hereunder is their compensation package:

You get paid 5 different ways:
1. Retail Sales – Online/Offline,
2. Fast Start Bonus 25%,
3. Binary Commissions and Cycle Bonuses,
4. Matching Bonuses,
5. Leadership Coding Bonuses.

You be the judge, Linear Income – exchange time for money, only get paid if you work, and get paid only on your own efforts versus Leveraged Residual Income – allows you to be paid on the efforts of hundreds if not thousands of others, get paid for a lifetime for work you did once, and get paid 24/7 even when you are sleeping.

The time has truly arrived when with the help of the Internet; the MLM industry should be revisited. I am fully aware that many will claim to suffer from MLM fatigue but success comes sometimes by sticking with a business/project that makes sense. Don't give up on a dream that can transform your life. The playing field has been leveled with the introduction of the internet. You can now build a global organization. Your market is no longer your country, it is now the world! You can find leaders around the world with the effective use of social media and really do great things. MLM is good for you!

Remember always to Keep the Faith, God is in Charge, Dream Big and expect Daily Miracles!

**Edward Harris**

# CHAPTER 16

## REAL ESTATE – A PLAYING FIELD FOR ACTIVE INVOLVEMENT - MULTIPLE STREAMS OF INCOME

Many small business persons miss out on opportunities to make passive income. One such area is Real Estate. My recommendation is that any business person who enjoys a reasonable degree of popularity should establish relationship with a Realtor and register as a Referral Agent. I have always maintained that possibilities for making money should not be ignored. It is unfortunate that most persons tend to treat lightly the efforts of persons who refer business to them. Sometimes the income resulting from a referral can be substantial.

The question that should be asked every time someone is involved in a deal that will generate income is – What is in it for me? Real Estate gives the greatest reward, whether you introduce someone seeking to sell a piece of land or a property comprising of house and land, or lease a property, or the opposite where someone is seeking to acquire or lease property. The commission on Sale of Property is 5% (can be negotiated downward) and on lease for a minimum of six months - equivalent of 1 month rent. The average property today costs approximately EC$500,000.00. The commission is EC$25,000.00. Rentals average around EC$2,000.00 per month. The commission is the equivalent of 1 month rent = EC$2,000.00. As a Referral Agent registered with a Broker, you are entitled to 25% of the gross, EC$6,250.00 and EC$500.00 respectively. Are you prepared to leave this amount of money on the table? I recommend to anyone who is in business to explore opportunities in the Real Estate sector and seek to establish a formal relationship with a reputable Real Estate Agent/ Broker/ Realtor.

In discussing opportunities for passive income, the MLM industry cannot be ignored. Chapter 15 deals with the Multi-level Marketing (MLM)/ Network Marketing/Relationship Marketing industry. This industry needs to be pursued and understood. It can be the next big wave in the Caribbean that can generate substantial employment opportunities and help alleviate poverty. Combining Real Estate with MLM can be a great fit.

Make effective use of your time, put technology to work for you. Seek out opportunities. Take a look at Affiliate Marketing and promote other company's product/s for a straight commission.

Set up a Facebook account and begin to build a list of friends. Establish a FB Page and begin to test your ideas and share your opportunities. It will be great to spend some time building a Free Website.
Try www.wix.com or www.freewebs.com

## ST. LUCIA! A UNIQUE DESTINATION
## FOR BUSINESS, PLEASURE AND RETIREMENT.

Welcome to St. Lucia! It is a small island State located between 60 and 61 degrees West Longitude and 13 and 14 degrees North Latitude, approximately 1,300 miles Southeast of Florida. St. Lucia is part of the archipelago in the Windward island chain. The 238 square mile island is 21 miles from Martinique its nearest neighbour which is a French Department, 24 miles North of St. Vincent and 100 miles Northwest of Barbados.

St. Lucia is such a prized jewel that it changed hands between the French and British 14 times before the French ceded their claim to the British in 1814. St. Lucia became an independent State on February 22, 1979 and retained the Queen as its titular head of State while maintaining a Westminster type Constitution which allows for good governance and a stable economy.

St. Lucia is more than simply beautiful. Her people are noted as some of the warmest and friendliest in the world. Her mountains have been and in some cases still are worshipped as demi-gods, adding to her mystery, her lure. Her waters offer safe swimming, excellent diving, and other water adventures such as kite surfing and parasailing. Land activities include but are not limited to games of golf, treks through the rain forest by land or zip line, horseback riding, turtle watching, spa treatments and more.

For many, this small and exotic island in the Caribbean has been inspirational. Oprah Winfrey mentioned it in her O magazine as one of the top 5 places to see in your lifetime. She is on to something, as in recent years St. Lucia has attracted some of the best developers in the world with International award winning plans that will cultivate and enhance St. Lucia's natural beauty. This is your invitation to Own A Piece of the Rock!

St. Lucia welcomes foreign direct investment, so there is nothing to fear in deciding upon St. Lucia as a destination whether for Business, Pleasure or Retirement or a combination of interests. It is important to note that St. Lucia is a preferred destination as it is evidenced by the heightened investment environment.

St. Lucia continues to strive to improve its ranking in the World Bank Report for "Ease of Doing Business. The Government has recently established an Economic Citizen Programme. St. Lucia is rated #1 Honeymoon Destination in the world. Visit http://www.stlucia.org Based on the foregoing information, it is evident that St. Lucia has all the attributes to fit the most discriminating life style. There is never a dull moment and the close proximity of neigbouring islands adds additional variety to the existing fun filled experience in St. Lucia. St. Lucia Jazz and Arts Festival in May and St. Lucia Carnival in July are two important events that attract thousands of tourists to the island annually.

In spite of the state of the Global Economy, the Real Estate market in St. Lucia has shown strong yield over time and continues to produce substantial returns for investors engaged in the sector. Prices for property in the North of the island continue to be attractive and have remained at the 2008/2009 level as in most parts of the island. Prices in the North range in the main between EC$22.00 and EC$41.00 while prices in the other parts of the island could be as low as 50% less. The challenge is to open up lands in the hinterland which beckons the future for serious developers.

The South of the island, for several years now, has been dubbed the New Frontier but so far real development is yet to make a major impact in that part of the island. However, all indications are that this is about to change, beginning with plans for the Hewanorra International Airport Development and other private and public sector initiatives within the construction sector. Apart from investment possibilities for acquiring independent residential and commercial properties, there are numerous opportunities to invest in Villa / Condominium Developments, and Boutique Hotels on the island.

In an interview with a prominent Realtor in the North of the island some years ago, she declared that "If St. Lucia was a young woman I imagine her putting her best clothes on, taking a deep breath and stepping out into the world. The world has taken notice!" She further stated that "St. Lucia is a young island in its development but it is all coming together now". That was then, some time has passed, but looking at things today, we can conclude that St. Lucia is poised to return to its former glory.

Here are a few important facts:

1.    That ownership of property by foreigners in St. Lucia is welcomed by the Government and citizens.
2.    That an Investor could be actively involved in the development of St. Lucia.
3.    That St. Lucia offers a life style suited to the most discriminating individuals.
4.    That St. Lucia is an Investor's Dream and it is all coming together now with its most recent launch of its Citizen by Investment Programme (CIP).

The Private Sector is well served by 7 seven Associations which allow Entrepreneurs to be fully engaged in matters that affect their sector. Corporate Social Responsibility is practiced by many companies. There are several service clubs such as Rotary and Lions which attract businesspersons who are conscious of their social responsibility.
If Island Living is your lifestyle choice, experience St. Lucia first hand, stay for a visit or for a while!!!

Article produced by: Edward A. Harris, Honorary Member – Realtors Association (St. Lucia) Inc. Business interests include: Real Estate, Business & PR Consulting, Networking & Freelance Journalism.

Websites: http://www.stluciaonestoprealtors.com
          http://www.stluciasimplybeautiful.com

# CHAPTER 17

## QUALIFICATION BY EXPERIENCE (QBE) RECOGNITION

Many Micro, Small and Medium Sized Businesses are owned and operated by Entrepreneurs 50 years and above. Fortunately, the services sector is slowly bringing young Entrepreneurs into the private sector. There is need for sharing the success stories which will encourage further involvement in the ICT and other technical areas. However, we must return to the foundation from which our business culture emerged. We owe a debt of gratitude to the trail blazers who by share will to succeed have established vibrant businesses and have left a rich legacy for all who will dare to take risks and be successful business persons. Those who made the difference qualifying themselves by experience through hard work and a burning desire to succeed should be recognized. Most of the times they did it alone. They have definitely earned the QBE certification.

Sole Proprietorship must mature and be taken to the next level of a registered company, paving the way for succession at the Board of Directors level. There was a time when it required two persons to form a Company. In recent times, the number was changed to one which in practice was what happened as the second person in most cases was the legal clerk in an Attorney's office with no interest in the company.

In considering the option for the formation of a Qualification by Experience (QBE) Association, I feel that there is an urgent need for a new approach to succession in family businesses and one of the programmes of the proposed Association should be the issue of Succession Planning - targeting the general membership. There is also the need for recognition of successful QBEs entrepreneurs which the Association when established must also seek to undertake.

I had the pleasure of being Chairman of a ceremony which was hosted by the Ministry of Commerce in Saint Lucia to honour three outstanding Entrepreneurs, one posthumously. During one of my remarks, I called on the gathering to ensure that the biographies of the three gentlemen be recorded for posterity. We need to preserve the legacies of those who have gone before and even those outstanding Entrepreneurs who are with us today. I must admit many are shy of their success.

It is time to take a look at how this terrible situation which has gone on for decades could be arrested. Over the years, many of entrepreneurs have educated their children with the hope that they will join them in the operations of their companies. Unfortunately, most of the young graduates have specialized in fields that are not consistent with the demands and expertise needed for the family business. The well trained family members who try to fulfill the dreams of their parents are in many cases frustrated by their philosophy and methods of doing business. The children are denied some of the basic perks which go along with Management positions and the salaries are usually substandard, with the parents treating them as children even though they hold positions of responsibility, claiming that the children will eventually own the business. These are some of the main reasons why most children take their exit and proceed to work outside of the family business. In some cases when succession in the management of the business fails to occur in a timely manner, the business is left to die a slow death and the life's work of the original owner/s is lost.

There is still a lot to be done but the most urgent need is for business people to get together, share experiences, take joint action among themselves to strengthen their businesses in areas of bulk buying, industry trends, best practices, quality control and social activities.
I feel eminently qualified to use the designation – QBE!

**Edward A. Harris, QBE**

# CHAPTER 18

## EDWARD A. HARRIS PROFESSIONAL EXPERIENCES & COMMUNITY INVOLVEMENT

Edward Alphonso Harris is Guyanese by birth, currently a nationalized Saint Lucian who has travelled extensively. He has lived and worked in several countries outside of his homeland, Guyana, including Barbados, Dominica, Grenada, Jamaica, Saint Lucia, Sierra Leone and Tanzania. He is tireless in his quest to share the Principles of Affirmation and to set alight the power of the Entrepreneurial Spirit as a means of assisting in alleviating poverty in the Caribbean and around the world.

As a child he helped in his mother's Parlour (Cake Shop), which was located on Water and New Market Streets in Georgetown, Guyana. Later, while still in his teens, he worked as a counter clerk at a pharmacy in Stabroek Market, a landmark location in the capital, Georgetown.

After a short stint in the Postal Service, where he got his first experience of job discrimination, with the encouragement of his uncles, he secured employment as a Counter Clerk with a leading grocery retail and diamond trading business in the interior of Guyana. In the first year, he was promoted to manage a branch shop and subsequently returned to the main office as Book Keeper.

Edward Harris began working at the tender age of fourteen and worked in his adult life almost entirely in the private sector in areas of manufacturing, distribution and services. At 73, he is not about to retire and is actively engaged in the areas of Business & PR Consulting, Real Estate, Networking, Freelance Journalism, Motivational Speaking and Private Sector Advocacy. Currently, he holds the position of General Manager for Essential Hardware Limited located in Vieux Fort, Saint Lucia.

Edward Harris founded the Guyana Association of Sales Personnel (GASP) in 1975 and the Guyana Small Business Association in 1989. In 1979, he sponsored the Castries Toastmasters Club and in 2007 he was elected Chairman of the Steering Committee which charted the course for the establishment of the Realtors Association (Saint Lucia) Inc. He was awarded the status of Honorary Member of the Association in May, 2010. He served the membership of the St. Lucia Industrial & Small Business Association (SLISBA) for sixteen consecutive years, during the period 1993-2009, in capacities as Secretary, Treasurer, President, Immediate Past President and Management Consultant.

Following is an abridged listing of his professional experiences, social and community involvement.

## ABRIDGED LISTING OF EXPERIENCES AND SOCIAL/COMMUNITY INVOLVEMENT

**Duration and Position:**

| | |
|---|---|
| 2009 – Present | Lead Consultant – Visionary Investment Consultants |
| 2007 – 2009 | Management Consultant St. Lucia Industrial & Small Business Association |
| 2004 | P.R. Consultant – Baron Foods Ltd. |
| 2004 – 2006 | P. R. Consultant – Destiny Group of Companies |
| 2003 - Present | Sales & Marketing Specialist, |
| 2003 – 2004 | Publisher/Managing Editor - The NetWorker Magazine |
| 2003 – 2010 | Owner-Broker–Eastern Caribbean Real Estate, Development Management Corp. |
| 1996 - Present | President - Millennium Investment & Consultants Brokerage |
| 1986 - 1999 | Executive Chairman - Chemical Manufacturing & Investment Co. |

| | |
|---|---|
| 1993 - 1999 | Chief Executive Officer - The Roserie Group of Companies |
| 1992 | Independent Service Provider Resource Consultant – Marketing - Caribbean Development Bank - C.T. C.S. - Network |
| January 1992 – February 1993 | Consultant - Gafsons Industries Limited & Gafoor and Sons Limited |
| January 1990-January 1991 | Consultant/Regional Marketing Manager - Intercorp Holdings Ltd., Comprising of: Stationery Manufacturers Ltd., Caribbean Chalks – Instruments and Art Products Ltd., Beautifit Career Fashions Ltd. |
| November 1981 – October 1983 | Sales and Marketing Manager (a) Gafsons Industries Ltd. (b) Barbados Steel Works Ltd. |
| October 1977 – April 1980 | Sales/Marketing Manager - Stanthur Company Limited |
| July 1975 – October 1977 | Sales Representative, Marketing Planner, Sales Manager, Berger Paints (Guyana) Ltd. |
| 1974 – 1975 | Sales and Circulation Manager - New Nation Papers Limited |
| 1973 – 1974 | Marketing Officer - Guyana Co-operative Wholesale Society, Limited |
| 1969 – 1973 | (a) Payroll and Statistics (b) Office Manager Windsor Manufacturing Co. Ltd |
| 1964 – 1969 | Sales Representative, Debit Manager, General Agent - Insurance Industry |

## GARMENT INDUSTRY EXPERIENCES - CONSULTANT

1987 - 1989    Consultant - Caribbean Apparel Management and Consultancy Limited. Assignments – St. Lucia, Jamaica, Sierra Leone, West Africa. Harris Fashions, Guyana

1969 – 1973    Payroll and Statistical Clerk, Office Manager Windsor Manufacturing Co. Ltd., Guyana

## SOCIAL/COMMUNITY INVOLVEMENT

1975 - 1976    Founder/President of Guyana Association of Sales Personnel.

1976 - 1977    Treasurer of the Georgetown Toastmasters Club – Guyana

1979    Sponsor of the Castries Toastmasters Club – St. Lucia

1989    Founder/President of the Guyana Small Business Association

1995 - 1996    Secretary – Rotary Club of St. Lucia – South.

1996 - 1997    President – Rotary Club of St. Lucia – South.

1996 - 2001    President – Association of Eastern Caribbean Exporters – Dominica.

1996 - 1998    Secretary/Treasurer – St. Lucia Industrial and Small Business Association

1998 - 1999    Secretary – Rotary Club of St. Lucia – South.

1999/2000    President – Rotary Club of St. Lucia – South.

1999/2000    Assistant District Governor – St. Lucia. District No. 7030 – Rotary.

2002/2003    President - St. Lucia Industrial & Small Business Association.

2001/2002    Patron of the St. Lucia Division of the Salvation Army.

2002/2003    Member of the Advisory Board of the St. Lucia Division of the Salvation Army.

2004 – 2006    President of the Guyana – Saint Lucia Association.

| | |
|---|---|
| 2005 – 2006 | Public Relations Officer for the Caribbean Association for Researchers and Herbal Practitioners (CARAPA). |
| 2007 – 2009 | Chairman, Steering Committee – Realtors Association |
| 2010 | Honorary Member - Realtors Association (Saint Lucia) Inc. |

Mr. Harris is available to make a presentation to students and groups who are interested in gaining further knowledge on any of the topics presented in this book. He could be contacted at jobfreelife72@yahoo.com.

You are invited to visit my Archive at
http://www.stluciasimplybeautiful.com

I am sincerely grateful to my friends Eric and Bjorn Tomme and their families of Belgium, and lovers of the Caribbean for keeping the website on line over the years. Eric is primarily responsible for introducing small hotels in St. Lucia to the World Wide Web (www) with great websites.

Check out their website at
www.cavip.com

# CHAPTER 19

## THE CONFIDENCE BUILDING EXERCISE – AFFIRMATION!

People always ask me how I get involved with so many different things and put so much energy into what I do. It is all about the WILL to achieve success. I affirm my desires every day. I live in faith and believe in my heart that "I can do all things through Christ which strengtheneth me" Philippians 4:13. Most people give lip service to this Biblical Affirmation. Affirmation is life transforming – converting negative to positive. Throughout my life I practiced this technique whether applied to my personal life or business. I can preach an entire sermon on this topic but for now, I will rather share with you how I apply the simple technique to ensuring success in my life, living in abundance and celebrating life!

## AFFIRMATION

MY GIFT TO YOU I am sharing with you a system that has worked miracles in my life. To many of you who will read this publication, you have been exposed in some way to this information but have done nothing with it. I believe that having read the foregoing pages, you are now ready to go forward in applying the principles of AFFIRMATION which I share with you hereunder:

I have used many techniques but Affirmation has given me the faith that I needed throughout the years. My first encounter with Affirmation was at the age of thirteen when my Sunday School Teacher (she was a member of the Anglican Church and an avid subscriber to the Unity community) gave me my introduction to Affirmation which was well put together on a piece of Bristol board. I pasted it on to my wardrobe and every morning as I prepared to step out to greet the fortunes of the new day, I would say my Affirmation aloud. As I looked into the mirror, regardless of the circumstance, I would smile because of my confidence in the Power of Affirmation.

The Affirmative statement was as follows:
"I am now eternally and forever almighty, all powerful and all wise. I am free, peaceful, loving, healthy, and happy, I am abundance and plenty, I am that I am, so be it, so shall it be, thank you Father God".

Those are powerful words! Then there is the sum total of the route to one's salvation.
"If thou shalt confess with thy mouth the Lord Jesus, and shalt believe in thine heart that God hath raised Him from the dead, thou shalt be saved." (Romans 10:9)

If you can speak it, you can have it. Dr. Denis Waitley speaks about SELF TALK and Napoleon Hill said "whatever the mind can conceive and believe it can be achieved."

Most good self help books speak to writing down the desires of your heart which is critical for actualisation. My technique includes speaking, writing, and more. Let us get into the habit of making a conscious effort of putting our mind to work. We must become big dreamers. We must conceptualize, visualize, and actualize our thoughts. Knowledge without action is just entertainment. So it is when we dream big and do nothing tangible, we just entertain ourselves. Little things mean a lot. Too many of us look for big things, signs and wonders.

Many lack faith. Affirmation is built on faith in possibilities that are beyond our current state of achievement. But you must begin your journey with small steps. Faith is defined in the Bible as the substance of things hoped for, the evidence of things not seen. With God all things are possible and I have concluded that nothing good happens without God. Now that I presume that we understand each other. I say with confidence that Affirmation works. It has worked for me and it will work for you. Just step out in Faith.

With pen and paper in hand, take the first step:

1.  Make a list of all the hindrances in your life - Owe the Bank, Having domestic problems, Not earning enough money, You get the drift – you can continue. Exhaust the list of negatives in your life.

2.  Make a list of all the things you need to achieve in life to fulfill your dreams. Need a proper education, Need a spouse, Need a job, Need to be a top Internet Marketer.

3.  Convert all the negative and positive statements into AFFIRMATIVE STATEMENTS. Be definitive about what you want to achieve.

For Example:

Need a job: I, John Jones by the 31st August, 2016 will land a job as the Executive Director of ABC Associates on Main Street, Castries, St. Lucia with my office located in Room 2 in the Hewanorra Tower, responsible for 50 employees and reporting directly to the Board of Directors, earning in excess of EC$300,000.00 per annum and taking care of my family – celebrating life.

The sky is the limit; never see yourself in the present. You took into consideration the date, the position, the salary and your intention to take care of your family. Do not limit yourself.

I always believe that the proof of the pudding is in the eating. I have had affirmation after affirmation realized in my life over the years. Each New Year's Eve, I commit myself to writing down a list of Affirmations that will get me to the place I want to be during the ensuing year. Every time, I surprise myself as to how much I achieved. Some years I updated the list several times.

Affirmation, gives you the opportunity to challenge yourself to take action to achieve the things you desperately want to achieve. Give yourself a head start with a Life Changing Technique that is simple in its application with amazing results! You have nothing to lose, everything to gain –

Give AFFIRMATION a try.

In business, you need direction, you need to be focused. Affirmation substantially increases your chances for success!

# CHAPTER 20

## RECOMMENDED WEBSITES

In recent years the Government of Saint Lucia has made advances in Information Technology (IT) and information is now available on several websites. The Private Sector has made use of IT with websites and Social Media. This enthusiasm for sharing knowledge and opportunities will expand into the future. As MSMEs operators you are now connected. When visiting any website, look for the suggested links on the site.

1.  www.google.com puts the world at your finger tips. Just ask any question in the Google Search Box and get the answer.
2.  www.govt.lc Check the links on this site and be informed about any area of government's involvement.
3.  www.stlucia.org Tourism is the principal export earner.
4.  www.investstlucia.com This is St. Lucia's window on investment.
5.  www.stluciajazz.org The home of St. Lucia Jazz & Arts Festival
6.  www.hiredcaribbean.com Employment Billboard
7.  www.businessforhome.org Updates on MLM Companies
8.  www.mlmwatchdog.com MLM Industry Updates
9.  www.maxsteingart.com/webinars Best MLM/Network Marketing Training
10. www.realtors.org Real Estate Portal
11. www.linkedin.com Professional Group
12. www.facebook.com/edharrisbiz Facebook Page #1 Social Media
13. www.youtube.com Information & Social Videos
14. www.twitter.com Source of Breaking News
15. www.stluciasimplybeautiful.com The archive of Harris at Large
16. www.brainstorminggroup.webs.com The Power of Affirmation and Goal Setting
17. www.stluciaonestoprealtors.com Real Estate Offerings
18. www.socialmediaexaminer.com Social media training
19. www.worldventures.com A MLM electronically delivered service

# CHAPTER 21

## MOVING FORWARD

The principal objective of the originator of this business training programme is to set up an institution that will seek to transform lives – socially and economically. Towards this end the phases of the project are highlighted hereunder:

**Phase 1 Launch of Publication:**
To foster the spirit of Entrepreneurship in our beloved country – Saint Lucia, and the wider Caribbean through the publication and distribution of my latest work which is a revisit to my earlier book "You Can Be A Successful Business Person" now renamed "WINNING STRATEGIES FOR MICRO, SMALL AND MEDIUM ENTERPRISES (MSMEs)" with six additional chapters.

Initially 1,000 copies will be printed. Copies of my book will be distributed FREE OF CHARGE to the 23 Public Secondary Schools and 16 Public Libraries.

**Phase 2 Lectures:**
Over the past several years, I have been invited to make presentations to 5th Form students on STARTING UP AND MANAGING A SMALL BUSINESS by the Student Counselor of the Vieux Fort Comprehensive Secondary School – Campus B. I have presented on Business Related topics to students of other learning institutions including Sir Arthur Lewis Community College.

In spite of business studies being included in the curriculum, there is still a lack of understanding about the role of the private sector and its contribution to the National Economy. Students are not even interested in working in the Private Sector, not even to use it as a stepping stone to equipping themselves financially or otherwise for further advancement of their career path.

**Phase 3** will see the establishment of a website – fully supported by Social Media that will not only promote "Winning Strategies for Micro, Small & Medium Enterprises (MSMEs)" but will also encourage local writers to take advantage of promoting approved books on the site.

**Phase 4** will give initial sponsors the opportunity to promote their products/services at concessional rates on a ½ hour TV/Radio programme with one of the leading media houses. This weekly discussion programme will afford Entrepreneurs an opportunity to share their business experiences while at the same time promoting their products.

**Phase 5** will see the establishment of The KNOWLEDGE SHARING INSTITUTE where an itinerant structure will be established to facilitate participants around the island. Life Skills and Entrepreneurship will be taught. Internet Marketing and Social Media will be an integral part of the project. Technology will be the driver of this project, using web base meeting platforms for training.

Entrepreneurs are invited to partner with me to share our experiences as we seek to transform the lives of our young and old, under employed and unemployed in our communities - island wide.

# CHAPTER 22

## CONCLUSION

It is my sincere hope that you enjoyed reading this book and that it has reinforced your understanding of the fundamentals for establishing a business within in the MSMEs sector. It is all about introducing you to Winning Strategies. My experiences included in the preceding chapters give testimony to the fact that I have walked the walk and now share my experiences with the world in the hope that in some way I will be able to contribute to the success of individuals seeking to start a business and even those who have progressed to the stage of being Entrepreneurs and are successful in their businesses. A special word to those who are struggling in their selected area of business, I invite you to review your current status against the suggestions I have made.

Here is something that I feel compelled to share with you. Mike Litman, author of Insider Secret revealed a secret that the wealthy and powerful have used throughout the ages to subject the poor and middle class to poverty, where the rich gets richer and the poor and middle class get poorer. He claimed that the proof lies in the fact that "3% of the world own 97% of the wealth". He further claimed: - 1. That ordinary people are blind to the secret of Selling and how leaders use words to create empire 2. That you can turn your words into multiple sources of income and make millions. People are miserable and desperate trying to find part time businesses of their own. "If you don't know how to sell you will never stop living from pay check to pay check hell." To them it is a four letter word FEAR. Poor and middle class are always in a state of financial chaos because they are afraid of Selling.

It was clear to me several years ago when I was introduced to scientific selling by the National School of Salesmanship where I received the Red and Gold Seal Diplomas that "EVERYONE NEEDS TO BE A SALESPERSON". Whether you realize it or not, you are on a sales crusade throughout your life working at convincing others, using the power of words. This knowledge can make the difference in your life in general and your business in particular. Sell, Sell, Sell!

To all my readers, I invite you to visit my group at
http://www.brainstorminggroup.webs.com
Please feel free to enter the discussions, share your experiences and business opportunities.
It is in sharing that you will receive. May you be blessed abundantly in your life and in your businesses!

GO AHEAD – BE YOUR OWN BOSS

YOU CAN BE A SUCCESSFUL BUSINESS PERSON BY UTILISING WINNING STRATEGIES!!!

YES YOU CAN!

# NOTES

# A SPECIAL OFFER

Upon completion of this book, you can earn a Certificate on
Entrepreneurship and Life Membership by simply applying to:-
The Co-ordinator – Knowledge Sharing Institute
Email: info@knowlegesharinginstitute.org


# SPECIAL NOTE

Edward Harris – Author/Publisher of
Winning Strategies for MSMEs is available for
Speeches, Lectures, Seminars and Coaching events.

Reservation for our 2 day Workshop on
Winning Strategies for Micro, Small and Medium Enterprises
can be arranged by contacting Ed Harris at
Email: info@knowledgesharinginstitute.org


Be first to know what is happening at
KNOWLEDGE SHARING INSTITUTE AT

www.knowledgesharinginstitute.org

www.ingramcontent.com/pod-product-compliance
Lightning Source LLC
Chambersburg PA
CBHW060635210326
41520CB00010B/1609